Dining Eti
& Table Manners
Making your Mark at Dining Experiences

Gerard Assey

Dining Etiquette & Table Manners
By
Gerard Assey
© Copyright 2022 by Author

Published by:
Gerard Assey
19/18, Palli Arasan Street
Anna Nagar East
Chennai - 600 102

ISBN: 978-93-92492-34-1

Table of Contents

Preface
Restaurant and Dining Skills- Mastering Table Manners

What are Table Manners? Simply put, they are a set of rules that govern the expectations of social and dining behavior in a workplace, group or society and are a visible sign that you are a polished and knowledgeable professional

The question constantly arises, "Why are table etiquette and table manners so very important?"

It goes without saying, that understanding proper table etiquette and practicing good table manners are in part of what makes us civil human beings.

We all observe how other people act and we make judgments, whether positive or negative, on their behavior. Our practice of table etiquette is a reflection of our "breeding", not in the sense of genetics, but in how we have been educated and brought up.

Table manners play an important part in making a favorable impression. They are visible signals of your manners, and therefore, are essential to professional success. Whether having lunch with a prospective employer or dinner with a business associate, your manners speak volumes about you, your social skills and confidence, leaving a lasting impression-good or bad. Therefore being familiar with the rules of dining etiquette and the manners at the dining table can help to increase your professionalism in unfamiliar situations.

Most interviewees wrongly get the impression that the meal that they are invited out to is a time to relax and chat it up with the interviewer. The actual truth is that when an organization hosts a meal during an interview, they are assessing how you conduct yourself, your knowledge of etiquette and standard dining practices, and they are also observing how you will conduct yourself when meeting with clients and higher-ups in the company. Employers need to be firmly convinced that you can represent them in social settings with customers, clients' colleagues and competitors. They will be watching your dining manners. So the focus is on the interview, not the food

In the forthcoming pages you will get to learn step by step, the right ways to carry and conduct yourself professionally at any event or at the dining table enabling you gain all the confidence required and stand out in a highly positive manner.

Business Meal Etiquette-Planning and Arrival
First Impressions Matter!

Let's begin with Planning the Event

Here are a few key etiquette tips on planning a business lunch if you are the host:

- ✓ What is the occasion? Formal/Informal?
- ✓ When are you planning to have it?
- ✓ Who are you planning to call?
- ✓ What are your guests likes/ dislikes, especially on the various cuisines? Ask when extending the invitation or give the guest a choice of two or three restaurants, if you have not yet decided on the same.
- ✓ Choose a restaurant that is not very far, that is convenient for all your guests, a restaurant you know well that has a diverse menu
- ✓ Make bookings in advance-Reserve a table/ room etc- indicate preference for seating (a spot that's quiet) Tell the person taking the reservation.
- ✓ Confirm the time and place and repeat the details of the invitation later in the conversation.
- ✓ Invite your guests well in advance (See details on the invitation below)
- ✓ Although invitations have traditionally been sent through the mail, invitations these days are through emails or WhatsApp or other electronic means, followed by a phone call, are becoming more acceptable.
- ✓ Make it clear that you are the host.

- ✓ Tell your guests what to expect so as to allow your guests to prepare in advance in case they have to bring anything along.
- ✓ Reconfirm the reservation at the restaurant/ hotel one or two days before the dinner has been planned.
- ✓ Reconfirm with your guest. Call on the morning of a lunch or dinner; if you've scheduled breakfast, call the day before.

Business Invitations-Content

A Business Invitation can be formal or informal, but must have the following:

The Company name and or logo,

The Names of the host/hostess,

Invitation Openings (the following are some suggested ones, depending on your company and the occasion),

- ✓ "you are cordially invited to"
- ✓ "requests the pleasure of your company at"
- ✓ "requests your presence at"
- ✓ "invites you to"
- ✓ "requests the honor of your presence."
- ✓ "cordially invites you to"

Nature of the event- State whether the event is for breakfast, lunch, or dinner, a cocktail party or some other occasion. (Mentioning this can help them plan accordingly)

What is the purpose? To celebrate a milestone, to introduce someone or a new product, to honor a retiree, or to celebrate an occasion or just another festive event

- ✓ Date and time of the event
- ✓ Place- The address of where the event will be held, ideally with a location map in case the guests have not been before.

- ✓ RSVP- the RSVP address or phone number is in the bottom left-hand corner of the invitation.
- ✓ Special instructions- On the right hand side bottom corner are any special instructions such as attire, parking instructions, landmarks of the location etc.
- ✓ Formal business invitations are based on the company culture, tradition etc, but it must eventually uphold and promote the company's image
- ✓ For a casual gathering, there may not be a need to have invitations printed. These could be on preprinted invitations, wherein you can simply fill the blanks by hand, of what, where, and when the party will be and who is hosting it.
- ✓ Some formal invitations include an RSVP notation and your phone number or contact details on the invitation.

Responding to the Invitation

- ✓ If you are one of the guests that have received an invitation, then you must respond accordingly
- ✓ You can use the address or phone number provided on the invitation or return the RSVP card that could have also been sent along with the invitation.
- ✓ However, if "Regrets only" is printed at the bottom corner of the invitation, then you would need only get back to the host if you are not be able to attend. If your host does not hear from you, you are expected to attend. If you see a "Please reply by" a given date in the invitation, be good enough to reply by that date.

✓ Remember, that it is not right to ask to bring a guest unless the invitation states "Mr. Fernandez and Guest", as food and beverages would have been placed only for the number of people invited- and thus you would be inconveniencing the host. If you don't want to go to the party or dinner without that special someone, decline the invitation. Let the host know that you'd like to get together with him at a time when your friend can accompany you, or when the associate isn't with you. If however, such a line is indicated in the invitation allowing you to bring in a guest, then you may fill in your guest's name and details required

Arriving at the Venue

Good dining etiquette and the impression you make on your business lunch partners/ companions starts when you first arrive at the restaurant.

✓ Never be late: By arriving even a few minutes late, you could leave a bad impression and send a clear message of carelessness and thoughtlessness. Be on time- no one wants to be kept waiting. If it is an unavoidable delay, try to contact the person. Keep in mind that you never know when you will encounter heavy traffic, road blocks, construction or other delays

✓ Dress appropriately. Dress according to the invitation or suggestion by the host. Check with the organizers/ host on the right dress code. If no dress code is indicated, assume business professional

- ✓ Remember to always say a "thank you" to the valet attendant as he takes your car and tip when your car is handed back to you after the event.
- ✓ When you are before the host: If you happen to arrive at the venue before the host, then the right etiquette dictates that you wait in the lobby or reception area for him/ her. It is not appropriate to move to the table and wait.
- ✓ When you are the host: If you are the host, it is appropriate for you to wait for your guest in the lobby. When some of your guests have arrived you can proceed to the table at the right reservation time, and have the maitre d' or waiter escort the other guests that follow later.
- ✓ Greetings and Introductions: When meeting someone, rise if you are seated, smile, extend your hand and repeat the other person's name in your greeting. A good handshake is important- it should be firm and held for three to four seconds
- ✓ These days, in most countries in the business world, it is not necessary to wait for a female to initiate the handshake. Females/males should both be ready to initiate the handshake. However, as a precaution check the respective cultures in countries/ organizations prior to the event.
- ✓ Another important act is the introducing of people in business life, yet few people know how to do it. Be sure to explain who people are and use their full names. Also do not assume that everyone wants to be called by

his or her first name - wait until you are told to use a first name
- ✓ When you arrive at the table: Remain standing until the host indicates to be seated. Wait until you are invited to be seated, or after the host first sits down.
- ✓ As a general rule, follow the lead of the host before removing your jacket. If the host keeps theirs on, keep yours on. If it is very hot weather, it is acceptable to ask their permission to remove your jacket. This applies to both men and women. Some restaurants may require that customers keep their jackets on during meals, depending on the occasion or event.
- ✓ Do not place any bags, purses, sunglasses, cell phones, or briefcases on the table.
- ✓ Women take purses to the table, where they're kept in the lap or at the feet.
- ✓ Packages, big bags, umbrellas, and other items are usually checked at the reception.
- ✓ Sit up straight; don't lean or place your elbows on the table
- ✓ Place Cards: It is not appropriate and bad manners to alter your place card setting. It has been prearranged by the host.

Duties of Gentleman and Ladies- Car, Door, Coats, Escorting

- ✓ Getting into a car: The gentleman will walk with the lady to the door closest to where she will be sitting. She waits as he opens the door for her. Ladies, always wait for a gentleman to open the door, as he is courteous. Ladies will sit down, backside first then swing her legs into the car (knees together). She will always say "thank you" to the gentleman. Don't forget to fasten up your seat belt!

✓ Exiting from a car: Once at the destination, the gentleman will leave the car and close his door. He will walk to the lady's door and open it. He will then give her his left hand to help her out of the car. He will close her car door. He will then give her his right arm and escort her to the event they are going to attend (dinner, movie, concert, restaurant, church, or party).

✓ When entering a building: Upon reaching the main entrance door to the event, they will drop escort arms and the gentleman will open the door for the lady. If the door opens forward, towards you, the gentleman will pull the door out, hold the door open, and let the lady pass through. If the door opens away from you, the gentleman will push the door open while walking through. He will then hold the door open while the lady walks through. If the door is a revolving door and it is already in motion, the lady will go through first and then the gentleman. If the door is a revolving door but it is not moving, the gentleman will push it forward, walking through, and the lady will follow him.

✓ Getting the Coat off, once Inside: The gentleman will offer to help the lady remove her coat. He will stand behind her and place both hands firmly on the back shoulders of her coat. She will slip her arms out while he guides her. (At some top class hotels you may be required to leave the coat in a coat claim room and leave it with the person watching the coats- the gentleman accompanying the lady must ideally assist with this). Usually, he will be given a token/ ticket with a number on it. He must give this back to the coat check person in order to be given the correct coat. It is expected that, if a coat checkroom is used and there is an attendant, you leave a small tip per coat. If no coat checkroom then the gentleman will carry the lady's coat to their table and place it on the back of her chair or on a hook nearby. Upon leaving, the gentleman will get the lady's coat, open the coat with both hands, and guide her into her coat. He will then put on his own coat

✓ Gloves: Ladies, if you are wearing gloves, take them off before going to the refreshment table and place them on your chair.

Before the Meal or Event

Before being seated
- ✓ Allow yourself some time before you actually get to your seat for freshening-up with a visit to the restroom.
- ✓ Check for the setting of your ties, bows, buttons undone, zippers, a belt that is not centered, tossed hair, earring off, smudged makeup etc.
- ✓ Turn off or keep all cell phones or other devices silent
- ✓ Place items such as purses, handbags, umbrellas, keys, or personal items under the table
- ✓ When meeting someone, rise if seated
- ✓ Smile and extend your hand, repeating the other person's name in your greeting
- ✓ A firm handshake should last three to four seconds. Both men and women should be ready to initiate the handshake.
- ✓ Do not remove your jacket unless the host does. If you are uncomfortable, you may ask the host permission to remove your jacket.
- ✓ It is considered acceptable for men to assist women with their chair but it does not always happen; in upscale restaurants, wait staff may assist.

Place Seating at a Formal Dinner
Here are some key rules for formal dinners:
- ✓ In a restaurant, the guest of honor should sit in the best seat at the table.

- ✓ Usually that is the one with the back of the chair to the wall.
- ✓ Once the guest of honor's seat is determined, the host should sit to the left.
- ✓ Other people are then offered seats around the table.
- ✓ The male guest of honor sits on the hostess' right
- ✓ The next most important man sits on her left.
- ✓ The female guest of honor sits on the host's right.
- ✓ The second most important woman sits on the host's left.
- ✓ Men and women should be alternately seated.
- ✓ Couples should ideally be separated.
- ✓ For this reason, use of round tables puts everyone on an equal basis.

Seating for Formal Dinners

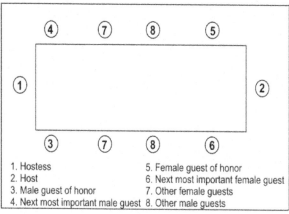

1. Hostess
2. Host
3. Male guest of honor
4. Next most important male guest
5. Female guest of honor
6. Next most important female guest
7. Other female guests
8. Other male guests

- ✓ Social manners are expected though nowadays not much practiced: males should seat females and rise when they leave and return to the table.
- ✓ There may be place cards at a formal dinner or your host/hostess may indicate where you should be seated. Your host may have seating arrangements in mind, so you should allow him to direct you to your seat. If you are the host, then you should suggest the seating arrangements.
- ✓ If in a group dining out for a meal and if there is an official host, then it's this host's responsibility to direct and guide the guests to their respective chairs. If he/she chooses not to, guests may ask where they should sit.
- ✓ At a table with a banquette, women are generally seated on the banquette along the walls, while the men on chairs opposite them.
- ✓ In earlier days, the host and hostess were usually required to sit opposite each other, and other couples split and mixed so they could have a chance to mix and converse with others. However these days, seating choices depend more on the preferences of each person and the occasion.

Posture and Poise at the Table
- ✓ Once seated at the Dinner Table, ensure that you sit up straight; do not slouch or lean over the table
- ✓ Your feet should rest flat on the floor; not crossed or wrapped around the chair legs.

- ✓ You may cross your ankles, but crossing legs causes slouching and makes you look too casual.
- ✓ Do not rock back in the chair.
- ✓ Keep your elbows off the table and left or right hand in your lap.
- ✓ Elbows on the table are only acceptable between courses when there is no plate in front of you. When you are not eating, keep your hands on your lap.

Your Posture at the Dining Table

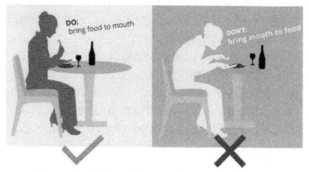

Sit up straight with your feet on the floor

When Ordering

Here are a few points to keep in mind when ordering:
- ✓ Once seated, take your napkin, fold it in half and place it on your lap. Again, wait staff may assist but it is appropriate to do this yourself. (See under another chapter later on the complete details of napkin etiquette)
- ✓ Avoid taking a lot of time to order as you could keep others waiting.

- ✓ Try not to complicate by customizing your order excessively as this can attract unnecessary and negative attention. The safest would be to follow your host's lead. Consider asking your host/hostess for a recommendation before making your decision.
- ✓ If you are the host, it is courteous to take the lead in ordering appetizers and wine, if these are to be served. Otherwise, do not order alcoholic beverages unless your host suggests or offers.
- ✓ If the host orders a bottle of wine and insists, only have ONE glass.
- ✓ Avoid foods that are difficult to eat like finger foods and/or are messy- like spaghetti, chicken wings, ribs, etc.
- ✓ If you are the guest, select an item that is in the mid-price range, easy to eat and one you will enjoy. Do not order more expensive meals or additional courses than your host.
- ✓ If you have questions about items on the menu, you can ask your server or host.

Serving
- ✓ Wait for everyone at your table to be served before beginning to eat. However, if an individual who has not been served as yet, but encourages you to begin eating, then you may do so.
- ✓ But remember to eat slowly while waiting for their food to be served
- ✓ At the Serving Table/ Buffet Service: A gentleman escorts a lady to the refreshment table. The gentleman asks the lady if she would like some refreshments. The lady may

answer, "Yes, please" or "no thank you". If the lady says yes, the gentleman picks up a plate and napkin, placing the napkin under the plate, and hands them to the lady. The lady then continues in the refreshment line and serves herself.

✓ The gentleman follows, getting his own plate and napkin and serves himself.

✓ The lady may stop at the beverage area and wait for the gentleman, who asks the lady if she would like some. Again, after the lady responds with "yes, please" or "no thank you", the gentleman picks up a cup and hands it to the lady, turning the cup so that the handle is towards the lady. A lady always expresses her appreciation. The gentleman will now pick up his own cup, and they walk back to their seats, side by side-but not in escort position. After refreshments, the gentleman may ask the lady if he may take her plate. He will carry dirty dishes to the service table. Dirty dishes are never returned to the refreshment table

Understanding the Table Setting before Beginning

Understanding the basics of table setting, can help you greatly in becoming an expert in the right dining skills. Depending upon the occasion, the placement of utensils could be "formal" or an "informal" table setting, and it's important to know how a table is set so that you could follow the proper table setting etiquette. Broadly, there are 4 Types of Table Settings:

- ✓ Basic
- ✓ Informal
- ✓ Formal
- ✓ Buffet

How utensils and tableware are placed on the table is very much like a road map that will indicate what type of a meal, the courses, and the beverages that will be served and how to go about it professionally. The right table setting for any event will depend on several factors, including: the formality of the event, how many courses to be served, and how it will be served.

So before we get into the various table settings, there are a few general table setting rules and guidelines that you must be familiar with:

- ✓ Table Cloth/ Mats: Although a formal dinner requires a tablecloth, at informal dinners a tablecloth is optional. A bare table with place mats is the alternative.
- ✓ Utensils: For starters, utensils are placed in the order in which they are used with the first ones placed on the outside. For example: the salad fork is placed on the outermost edge of

the left side before the dinner fork. This is because salads are usually served before the main course.

✓ A charger plate, also known as a service plate or under-plate, is a decorative base setting used during each dining course at weddings, banquets, or fine-dining establishments. Each course is served in a separate bowl or plate and placed on top of the charger plate. A charger plate is larger than a dinner plate but smaller than a serving platter.

✓ Forks: These are usually on the left side of the main service plate. The exception is the dessert fork which is above (top of) the plate and the oyster fork which is on the right side.

✓ Knives: Knives are always on the right side of the plate, with the cutting blade facing inwards towards the plate. The exception is the butter knife which is on the butter plate, (the butter plate is placed at the left top of the main service plate) with the blade pointing downwards and left.

✓ Spoons: Spoons are typically on the right side of the plate. The exception is the dessert spoon which is directly above (at the top of) the service plate.

✓ Placement: All utensils are usually about an inch from the edge of the table and lined up evenly from the bottom ends.

✓ Salt and Pepper: Since most people are right-handed, the salt shaker is placed to the right of the pepper shaker, in a position closer to the right hand, with the placement of the pepper shaker to the left of the salt shaker. Because salt is finer than pepper, the lid of the

salt shaker is punctured with smaller, more numerous holes than a pepper shaker.
- ✓ Only what is used depending on the event, is usually placed on the table: Eg; If there is no soup, there's no soup spoon placed.
- ✓ Coffee cups are to the right of the knife and spoon

Remember, it is never a good idea to finger around or rearrange the silverware or glassware placed in front of you

Basic Table Setting Items:

At the Center
- ✓ Service plate: The service plate, or entrée plate, is on top of the charger (if one is provided-though in most basic settings it may not), and is usually taken away before the next course.
- ✓ Napkin: The napkin is folded and on top of the plate before service begins.
- ✓ Menu card: The menu card is either on top of the napkin or inserted into the folds of the napkin for a more formal display.

At the Left-side
- ✓ Salad fork: Salad is the second course that is served, so the salad fork is at the outer left edge of the table setting. The salad fork is usually smaller than the dinner fork.
- ✓ Dinner fork: The dinner fork is to the immediate left of the charger or service plate. The dinner fork is typically the largest fork.

At the Right-side
- ✓ Soup spoon: Soup is typically the first course that is served. Therefore, the soup spoon is on the outer edge of the right side.

- ✓ Dinner knife: The dinner knife is to the immediate right of the service plate, corresponding with the placement of the dinner fork.

At the Top (above the service plate)
- ✓ Water glass: This glass is the largest of the glasses.
- ✓ Wine glass: A single wine glass is all that will be provided for a basic table setting, if wine is on the list for the event or function.

Informal Table Setting Items:

At the Center
- ✓ Service plate: The service plate, or entrée plate, is on top of the charger (if one is provided), and is usually taken away before the next course.
- ✓ Napkin: The napkin is folded and on top of the plate before service begins.
- ✓ Menu card: The menu card is either placed on top of the napkin or inserted into the folds of the napkin for a more formal display.

At the Left-side
- ✓ Salad fork: Salad is the second course that is served, so the salad fork is at the outer left edge of the table setting. The salad fork is usually smaller than the dinner fork.
- ✓ Dinner fork: The dinner fork is to the immediate left of the charger or service plate. The dinner fork is typically the largest fork.

At the Right-side
- ✓ Soup spoon: Soup is typically the first course that is served. Therefore, the soup spoon is on the outer edge of the right side.

- ✓ Salad knife: The salad is served after the soup, so the salad knife is to the left of the soup spoon.
- ✓ Dinner knife: The dinner knife is to the immediate right of the service plate, corresponding with the placement of the dinner fork.

At the Top (Above the Service Plate)

- ✓ Dessert teaspoon: This is above the entrée plate and is the smallest of the spoons.
- ✓ Water glass: This glass is the largest of the glasses.
- ✓ Wine glass: A single wine glass is all that you will find for an informal table setting.

The Various Table Settings

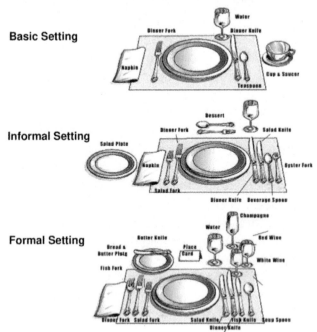

Very Formal Table Setting Items
At the Center
- ✓ Charger or Main Service Plate: The charger is the center stage of the table setting. As various courses come and go, these are set on top of the charger, including the salad course, soup course, and fish course. When the dinner course arrives, the charger is taken away.
- ✓ Service plate: The service plate, or entrée plate, is placed on top of the charger, and is usually taken away before the next course.
- ✓ Napkin: The napkin is folded and placed on top of the charger before service begins.
- ✓ Menu card: The menu card is either placed on top of the napkin or inserted into the folds of the napkin for a more formal display.

At the Left-side
- ✓ Salad fork: Salad is the second course that is served, so the salad fork is placed at the outer left edge of the table setting. The salad fork is usually smaller than the dinner fork.
- ✓ Fish fork: Next to the salad fork is the fish fork. In a formal setting, the fish or seafood course is served after the salad. Traditionally, the shape of the fish fork is designed to optimally lift the flesh away from the bones. In a dinner without a seafood course, the fish fork is used as the second course fork.
- ✓ Dinner fork: The dinner fork is placed to the immediate left of the charger or service plate. The dinner fork is usually the largest of the three forks.

At the Right-side

- ✓ Soup spoon: In a formal service, soup is the first course that is served. Therefore, the soup spoon is placed on the outer edge of the right side.
- ✓ Salad knife: The salad is served after the soup, therefore the corresponding knife is placed to the left of the soup spoon.
- ✓ Dinner knife: The dinner knife is to the immediate right of the service plate, corresponding with the placement of the dinner fork.

Above the Service Plate (Top)
- ✓ Butter plate: This plate is at the top left corner of the place setting.
- ✓ Butter knife: This is on top of the butter plate, pointing left with the blade facing down so that the handle is towards the guest.
- ✓ Dessert teaspoon: This is above the entrée plate and is the smallest of the spoons.
- ✓ Dessert fork: This is beneath the desert teaspoon, and can be used for the fruit course.
- ✓ White wine glass: The white wine glass is placed closer to the guest, as it is usually served before the red wine, along with the second course.
- ✓ Red wine glass: The red wine glass is larger and taller than the white wine glass.
- ✓ Champagne flute: The champagne flute is placed to the outer right of the glasses, because it accompanies the first toast.
- ✓ Water glass: This glass is the largest of the glasses, and is placed closest to the guest directly above the knives.

A Typical Buffet Setting

The buffet setting includes only the very essentials, and usually there will not be a plate or charger placed on the table, as the plates are usually picked up at the buffet table for the guests to serve themselves.

At the Buffet Table

- ✓ Service Plate and Napkin: Plates and Napkins are usually at the buffet table at the start of the buffet line. Sometimes each of these are just placed on each ones table in the center.
- ✓ Menu card: This is either in the form of a formal display, that spells out the items on the buffet table or alternatively, the name and description of each dish is on a label placed near the respective dish

At the Left-side

- ✓ Salad fork: Salad is the second course that may be had, so the salad fork is at the outer left edge of the table setting. The salad fork is usually smaller than the dinner fork.
- ✓ Dinner fork: The dinner fork is to the immediate left of the charger or service plate. The dinner fork is typically the largest fork.

At the Right-side

- ✓ Soup spoon: As soup is typically the first course, the soup spoon is on the outer right edge of the table setting.
- ✓ Dinner knife: The dinner knife is to the immediate right of the service plate, corresponding with the placement of the dinner fork.

At the Top

- ✓ Water glass: This glass is the largest of the glasses.

✓ Wine glass: A single wine glass is all that's needed for the buffet table setting, if it is part of the menu.

Note: Sometimes the entire cutlery mentioned above is placed on the buffet table and not on individual tables, along with the plates and napkins- in very informal settings, where each one helps themselves to whatever cutlery is required

How to work through the setting:
The best way to know how to work through the place setting, is to remember the basic rule, that all silver or glassware are arranged in the order a person will need to use them- and you must always begin from the outside. Solids are always placed to the left, while Liquids are always to the right. In order to remember the order, think BMW: Bread plate on the left, Main course in the middle, and the Water on the right. Start to use utensils on the outside first and work your way inward.

So, as an example, if you are served a salad first, use the fork set to the far left of your plate. Therefore the salad knife and fork (or the soup spoon if soup is served first) will be used first, then you will move towards the plate and continue with the main course by using your dinner knife and fork.

If dessert is ordered, you must then use your dessert fork and spoon located horizontally just above the main plate.

Your water glass is the one above the knife in your place setting and your bread plate is to the left. Sometimes the cutlery may be too close to the one seated next to you and you could be confused as to, whose bread plate or glass it belongs to. To help you through this confusion, remember "b" and "d". As you touch the index finger on your left hand to your left thumb, the "b" formed by your left hand is for "bread" (your bread plate is always to the left of your place setting). And as you touch the index finger on your right hand to your right thumb, the "d" formed by your right hand is for "drink" (your drinking glasses are always at the right of your place setting).

Remembering the Placements

The letter' **'b'** to remind of:
Bread (Solids)

The letter' **'d'** to remind of:
Drinks

More on this in the following chapters

The Various Course Meals

Meals are divided into courses, which refers to items served together at once. For example, soup and crackers are a course; so also are a salad, dressing, and bread served together. There is usually a pause in between courses, and the parts of a meal are brought out in a specific order. For example, if you order dessert and a main dish, two examples of courses, then your entrée will arrive before the dessert unless you specify you want a different order. Full course meals are made up of three courses: an appetizer, main dish, and dessert. Also known as a three-course meal or a standard course meal, you will sometimes see restaurants offering a full menu with these three items. You can add more courses to a full course meal.

Here are some examples of the different types of full course meals with the appropriate dishes listed:

- ✓ A single-course meal includes only a main dish or entrée.
- ✓ A two-course meal serves either a soup/salad followed by an entrée or a main course and finishes with a dessert item.
- ✓ Three-course meals have an appetizer, an entrée, and dessert.
- ✓ A four-course dinner includes a soup, salad, entrée, and dessert.
- ✓ Five-course meals serve an appetizer, soup, entrée, dessert, and cheese, or Soup, Fish, Main course, Dessert and Cheese or Soup, Appetizer, Salad, Main course and Dessert
- ✓ A six-course meal offers hors-d'oeuvres, soup, fish, and an entrée, followed by salad, coffee,

and dessert or Amuse-bouche, Soup, Hors d'oeuvres, Main course, Salad, Dessert or Appetizer, Soup, Fish, Salad, Main Course, Dessert

Here is an example of a classic French eleven-course meal including typical dishes for each course in brackets:
- ✓ First course- appetizer (green salad, smoked salmon)
- ✓ Second course- soup (cream of tomato, minestrone)
- ✓ Third course- fish (salmon, trout)
- ✓ Fourth-course- entrée (steak tartare, chicken breast)
- ✓ Fifth course- meat joint (roast leg of lamb-to work with a lamb wine pairing)
- ✓ Sixth-course- sorbet (lemon sorbet, raspberry sorbet)
- ✓ Seventh-course- roast (roast chicken, roast duck)
- ✓ Eighth-course- vegetables (spinach, broccoli, asparagus)
- ✓ Ninth-course- sweets (apple slices)
- ✓ Tenth-course- savory (crab cakes, spring rolls)
- ✓ Eleventh-course- nuts (walnuts, almonds)

Important to keep in mind are the Key Rules for a Balanced Menu
- ✓ A well-balanced menu does not duplicate taste. When cheese is served as an hors d'oeuvre, it is not incorporated in a dish served at the table.
- ✓ Because sweet foods dull the appetite, fruit is not served as an appetizer. The exception is

grapefruit, which has a sharp taste that stimulates the palate.

✓ When a first course is served in a pastry shell, dessert with a crust is not appropriate.

✓ If creamed soup is served as a first course, creamed vegetables are not included in the main course.

✓ When sauce is served, it is presented only once.

✓ From light to heavy, sour to sweet, each course is designed to meet a specific taste requirement.

Proper Utensil Etiquette
Handling the Tools of the Table

Your safest means of adhering to proper etiquette at the table would be to always follow the rule of "outside-in", as this will indicate to you, as to which knife, fork, spoon or other piece of cutlery to use at the dinner table. So always start with utensils on the outside first and work your way inward with each new course that is served. However, if you are still unsure, then just follow the host/ hostess in what they do.

Holding your Silverware: There are only two correct ways to hold and two ways or styles to use your silverware. Using your knife and fork, practice the two different methods described below and determine which one is most comfortable.

- ✓ Pencil Method: Hold the utensil like you would a pencil. It should be resting between the tips of your pointer finger and middle finger with your thumb on top to hold it in place. The end of the utensil should be resting on the webbing of your hand.
- ✓ Scalpel Method: Hold the utensil like you would a surgeon's scalpel. The tines of the utensil should face downward. Your pointer finger will press on the back of the neck and the end of the handle should be touching the center of your palm. Your remaining fingers grasp the utensil to hold it in place.

American Style vs. Continental Style
American Style
- ✓ Hold your fork like a pencil, with the shank extended between your thumb and index and middle fingers.
- ✓ Your fourth and fifth fingers rest in your hand.
- ✓ For leverage, the index finger is extended along the back of the fork, as far from the tines as possible.
- ✓ Hold the knife with the handle cupped in the palm of your left hand, along with your third, fourth, and fifth fingers.
- ✓ Place your second finger on the back of the blade.
- ✓ Hold your thumb against the side of the handle.
- ✓ Cut your food.
- ✓ Then place your knife down (blade facing toward you).
- ✓ Now switch your fork to the other hand and eat with the tines facing up

The most common method used in America is this method- you will hold your fork in your left hand, cut bite size pieces with your knife in your right hand, set the knife down on your plate, and transfer the fork to your right hand and eat. This is called the Zig Zag Method or American Style.

Continental Style
- ✓ Hold your fork in your left hand, tines downward.
- ✓ Hold your knife in your right hand, an inch or two above the plate. Extend your index finger along the top of the blade.

✓ Use your fork to spear, cut food and lift the food to your mouth. Do not switch hands. Continue to hold both utensils while taking a bite with the tines of the fork downwards. You can use your knife as a tool to position food on your fork.

As explained in the Zig-Zag Method above, use the utensils in the same hands as explained, but use your left hand to put food into your mouth. Either way, never cut more than 1-2 bites at a time. This is also called the European Method

Important Points to Note:

The continental style prevails at all meals, formal and informal, because it is a natural, non-disruptive way to eat.

If you are a slow eater, it is best recommended that the European method be used to speed up the process. If you are a fast eater, then the American method is best recommended to slow down the process.

Resting Position-Not Finished Yet!

When you take a break during your meal- to take a sip of your beverage or to speak with someone, rest your utensils in one of the two following styles:

✓ American Style: To show your server that you are NOT finished eating in the American style of dining rest your knife on the top right of your plate (diagonally) with the blade of the knife facing towards you and the fork nearby (tines up).

✓ Continental Style: To show your server that you are NOT finished eating in the continental style of dining, place your knife and fork on your plate near the center, slightly angled in an inverted V and with the tips of the knife and fork pointing toward each other. Make sure the tines of the fork are facing DOWN towards the plate in the Continental Style.

Resting Position

American Style
Resting Position

Continental Style
Resting Position

Finished Eating Position

When each course is finished:

- ✓ When you have finished eating, the fork and knife must be placed parallel to each other at the 4 O'clock or 10.20 position as if your plate were a clock.
- ✓ Make sure the blade of your knife is facing towards you and the tines of the fork face up in the American Style while the tines are down in the Continental position.

Finished Position

American Style
Finished Position

Continental Style
Finished Position

- ✓ This signals to the wait staff that you are finished.
- ✓ Always leave your dishes in place and let the wait staff remove them. Do not push plates away from you.

Other Dishes and Cutlery
- ✓ Soup spoons, coffee spoons, and dessert spoons should be placed on the service plate or saucer when you are finished eating. Never leave them in the bowl or cup.
- ✓ Never wave, or point using cutlery when you talk.
- ✓ Don't draw on the table cloth with anything, including utensils.
- ✓ Don't scrape the pattern off the plate.
- ✓ Never use your fingers to push food into your spoon or fork.
- ✓ When you are finished eating, don't push your plate away or stack your dishes.
- ✓ Never place used silverware back on the table.
- ✓ If a piece of silverware falls on the floor, do not go fishing for it. Simply push it under the table and discretely ask the server to bring you another one

Using Chopsticks
In most South East Asian countries, chopsticks are the traditional eating utensils, and knowing how to use them can add to your enjoyment of Asian cuisine. Each culture however, has their own set of table manners, though there are some general rules that will usually apply whenever you're eating with chopsticks. These are a pair of tapered sticks that are used as the primary eating utensils and are

usually made of wood, bamboo or plastic. You can also find chopsticks made out of metal, bone, and ivory. If you've never used chopsticks, at first it may seem awkward, but to start out you could practice at home using a pair of pencils if chopsticks aren't available.

Here are the steps to holding your chopsticks:

1. Hold one of the chopsticks in the groove between your thumb and fingers, by resting the chopstick on the end of your third finger (ring finger), while pressing gently with the lower part of the thumb to keep the chopstick in place.

2. Now hold the other chopstick with your thumb and first two fingers, as you would normally hold a pencil. The upper end of the chopstick rests in the groove, against the side of your first finger. The lower end rests against the end of your second finger. The tip of your first finger presses down on top of the chopstick for control, while you hold the lower end of the chopstick and your thumb steady

3. Now, using your first two fingers move the upper chopstick up and down, to grip small pieces of food between the two chopsticks. The index and middle fingers do the lifting. Use the index and middle fingers to close chopsticks over food. When moving the chopsticks, note that it is the top chopstick that should be moving, while the bottom should generally be still. If performed properly, you should be able to grasp small objects such as beans or grains of rice one at a time.

Using Chopsticks

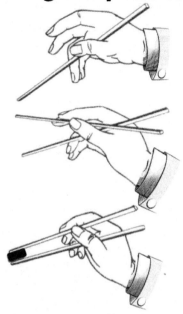

Chopsticks must always be kept in a parallel position- avoid crossing them.
Chopsticks can be used in many ways: To eat rice, dumplings, noodles, pasta, to stir soups and stews, picking up foods like meat, chicken, popcorn etc

What not to do with chopsticks
- ✓ Rest your chopsticks upright on the edge of a bowl
- ✓ Use your chopsticks to pull dishes toward you
- ✓ Pass food from chopstick to chopstick.
- ✓ Leave them stuck into a bowl of rice,
- ✓ Point your chopsticks at fellow diners

Napkin Etiquette
Here are some quick points to keep in mind about napkin etiquette:

- ✓ During informal meals, place the napkin in your lap immediately upon seating.
- ✓ When dining with others, place your napkin on your lap after everyone at your table has been seated.
- ✓ For formal occasions, before unfolding the napkin, wait for the host/ hostess to remove his/her napkin from the table and unfold it in his/her lap. The host leads in placing the napkin. Follow the lead.
- ✓ In some restaurants the waiter will place your napkin on your lap for you. You can be prepared by observation.
- ✓ Do not open your napkin in mid-air; as you remove your napkin from the table begin to open below the table level and place on your lap. The napkin should be folded and placed on your lap with the fold/ crease towards you.
- ✓ A small napkin may be opened fully. A large dinner napkin should be kept folded in half with the fold toward you. The size determines how you unfold a napkin in your lap. Large napkins are unfolded halfway, while the smaller napkins are unfolded completely and cover the lap fully.
- ✓ If a napkin ring is present, after removing your napkin, place the ring to the top-left of the setting. At the end of the meal, grasp the napkin in the center, pull it through the ring, and lay it on the table with the point facing the center of the table.
- ✓ Never tuck the napkin into your clothing, either at the waist, chin or into the collar of your shirt.
- ✓ If a napkin falls on the floor, politely ask the server to bring you another one.

- ✓ Do not wipe off cutlery or glassware with your napkin. If dishes aren't clean, ask the waiter quietly for replacements.
- ✓ Never use a napkin as a handkerchief or a bib. The napkin is used to blot your mouth, not serious wiping, and never for blowing your nose. If you must blow your nose, please excuse yourself from the table.
- ✓ For ladies, if you are concerned about your lipstick coming off on your napkin, blot it with a tissue before you come to the table. Lipstick on napkins or glasses is very unprofessional.
- ✓ If you need to excuse yourself from the table, temporarily, to go to the washroom or elsewhere leave your napkin on your chair. It is a sign to the hotel staff, that you are coming back and not to clear your table. If the chair is upholstered, place the napkin soiled side up.
- ✓ When the meal is over, loosely fold your napkin put it to the left of your place setting, and never on top of the plate. Keep your napkin in your lap until you leave the table. The host should be the first to put the napkin on the table at the conclusion of the meal. The most appropriate time to do this is as everyone is rising from the table
- ✓ If after-dinner coffee is served, then the napkin still remains on your lap.

Managing Basic to Formal Dining

Understanding a few Cutlery Rules are Key to your Success:

- ✓ Rule 1: The number of utensils indicates the number of courses. Most formal dinners will have multiple courses and typically, formal settings have seven courses: soup, fish, sorbet, a meat or fowl dish, salad, dessert and coffee.
- ✓ Rule 2: Begin with the outer utensils and work your way in. Sometimes, a utensil will be provided at the time of the specific course.
- ✓ Rule 3: Once utensils have been used, they do not lean on a plate or touch the table

Soup Etiquette

- ✓ Wait for everyone to be served, and then follow the host's lead to start.
- ✓ The soup spoon is provided by your waiter or it is on the table sitting to the right of teaspoon.
- ✓ Hold the spoon with thumb across the top of the handle, not with the handle in palm of hand.
- ✓ When eating soup, think of making a circle. Spoon away from you, bring it back around to your mouth and then back to the bowl. Dip soup spoon into soup moving away from you.
- ✓ Do not fill the entire spoon. Soup is taken from the side of the spoon so it is NOT inserted into your mouth. Sip from the edge of the spoon only- do not place the whole spoon in your mouth.

- ✓ Do not slurp or gulp or make slurping noises.
- ✓ To finish the soup, tilt the bowl away from you and use the spoon.
- ✓ When finished, rest spoon on saucer/platter. If no saucer, put the spoon on the plate under the bowl.
- ✓ Place crackers in soup only when at home alone with blinds down. Otherwise crackers should always be eaten with soup, not in soup.

Bread and Butter

- ✓ This plate is to the left of your dinner plate and above your forks. If you don't have a separate plate, it's okay to place the bread on your dinner plate.
- ✓ Bread is most often placed on the table in a basket that everyone shares.
- ✓ Because butter is produced in rectangle or square form, the butter knife is made with a dull blade to slice butter and a pointed tip to transfer cubes of butter to the plate.
- ✓ Place the bread and butter on your butter plate- yours is on your left
- ✓ Transfer butter or dips to your own plate instead of directly to the bread.
- ✓ Do not take bites directly from the roll. Tear off bite size pieces, butter them, and then eat them. Bread and rolls should never be eaten whole. Break into smaller, more manageable pieces, buttering a few bites at a time. Do not cut rolls or bread with a knife.
- ✓ Never completely cover it in butter, and do not stuff it all in your mouth at once - take small bites.

- ✓ Toast and garlic bread, however, may be eaten as whole pieces since they are usually already buttered.
- ✓ If served a hot muffin or biscuit, you may break in half crosswise, add butter, and put it back together. When ready to eat it, break it into small pieces
- ✓ In some restaurants, olive oil is served with bread. Dip your bite-sized pieces of bread in the oil and eat.

Passing Bread to Others
- ✓ If the bread is placed in front of you, feel free to pick up the basket and offer it to the person on your right.
- ✓ If the loaf is not cut, cut a few pieces, offer them to the person to your left, and then pass the basket to your right.
- ✓ Do not touch the loaf with your fingers- instead use the cloth in the bread basket as a buffer to steady the bread as you slice it.
- ✓ Don't hold your bread in one hand and a drink in the other
- ✓ Don't take the last piece of bread without first offering it to others.
- ✓ If a loaf of bread is served, the person the loaf is sitting in front of should cover the loaf with a clean napkin before cutting and pass the loaf to the right.

Seasonings and Sweeteners
- ✓ Always taste your food first before using any seasonings. Do not assume it needs to be seasoned.

- ✓ Do not be excessive with sugar or sweetener packets. The rule of thumb is no more than two packets per meal.
- ✓ Do not crumble the packets but partially tear off a corner, empty the contents and place to the side

Salads
- ✓ The salad plate is either to the left of your napkin or on top of your dinner plate.
- ✓ The salad plate is typically smaller than the dinner plate, but larger than the bread plate.
- ✓ It is perfectly acceptable to cut your salad. Ideally, the salad will be prepared so that it consists of bite-size pieces. If not, use your salad fork to cut them into smaller pieces. And if that does not work, you may use your dinner knife.
- ✓ Cut lettuce with your knife if necessary.
- ✓ Be careful with the cherry tomato, pierce it gently and cut it before placing in your mouth
- ✓ Make sure to keep your dinner knife for the main course.
- ✓ If an item falls of the plate, pick it up with a utensil and place it on the edge of the plate- do not eat it.

Sorbet
- ✓ Sorbet may be served immediately before the main course. This serves as a palate cleanser, so that you can appreciate the flavors of the main entrée.

How best to enjoy various food items-Fingers, Fork, or Spoon

- ✓ Artichoke: Use fingers to pull each leaf to dip in butter
- ✓ Asparagus: Fingers
- ✓ Bananas: Fingers
- ✓ Berries, melons, and grapefruit: Spoon
- ✓ Brownies and cookies: Fingers
- ✓ Cake: Can be broken and eaten like bread or crackers, or it may be eaten with a Fork.
- ✓ Celery, Carrot Sticks: Fingers
- ✓ Celery, olives, radishes, salted nuts, bonbons, preserved ginger and other trifles: Fingers
- ✓ Cheeses (Soft): Fork
- ✓ Cheese Cubes: Fingers
- ✓ Chips: Fingers
- ✓ Corn on the Cob: Fingers
- ✓ Crispy bacon: Fingers
- ✓ Cut fruit in a plate: Fork
- ✓ Dinner Rolls: Fingers
- ✓ French Fries (at the dining room): Fork
- ✓ French Fries (fast-food, picnic): Fingers
- ✓ Fried Chicken (dining room): Fork
- ✓ Fried Chicken (picnic): Fingers
- ✓ Grapes, plums, cherries, apples, peaches and other whole fruit: Fingers
- ✓ Ices, stiffly preserved fruits, etc: Fork.
- ✓ Lump sugar: Fingers, if no tongs provided
- ✓ Onion rings: Fingers
- ✓ Pizza: Fingers
- ✓ Potato: Use the Fork to break up a potato on your plate; do not use the knife.
- ✓ Sandwiches, Hot Dogs and Hamburgers: Fingers
- ✓ Spaghetti: Fork and Spoon

- ✓ Strawberries or dessert: Fork
- ✓ Sushi: Japanese eat with Fingers –so it's best to follow that way!
- ✓ Tacos: Fingers
- ✓ Watermelon: Fork

Twirling and Eating Noodles:
Hold the fork in your right hand (for a right handed person) as if you are going to poke the noodles. Take a small amount of noodles on the fork (less than you think you will need) and raise it out of the bowl to separate it from the rest of the noodles. Put the tines of the fork at an edge of the plate or bowl that is free of food. Point the tines of the fork straight down toward the plate. Then twirl the fork to wrap the noodles around the tines. When the noodles are wrapped all around, quickly pick up the fork with the rolled noodles around it and place it in your mouth.

Some key points to remember:
- ✓ When you pick up your food to take a bite, place the remainder back on your plate while you chew. Don't hold onto it and wave around during conversation.
- ✓ Keep your napkin ready, for wiping your hands, fingers, and blotting your mouth often.
- ✓ When using sauces, place an appropriate amount on your plate in which to dip your food. This helps eliminate double-dipping into the serving dish.
- ✓ When enjoying a burger, always cut it in quarters if it's very thick.

As You Start Eating, you must keep these points in mind

- ✓ If it is a small table of only two to four people, then you will need to wait until everyone else has been served before starting to eat. At a formal or business meal, you should either wait until everyone is served to start or begin when the host asks you to. You may begin eating when the host/hostess picks up their utensils.
- ✓ Remember that business meals are not about the food- they are about business first.
- ✓ Take small bites and never speak with food in your mouth- always finish chewing before speaking. Close your mouth while eating and never make noises when you eat. If a question is asked of you mid-bite, take a moment to chew and swallow your food. It is better to speak after a few seconds than to immediately blurt out your answer with a mouth full of food. Pace your eating. Pay attention to how fast or slow the other diners are eating so you do not finish way ahead of them or lag behind.
- ✓ If a piece of food happens to slip off your plate, discreetly place it back on the corner of your plate. If it is a small piece of food or salad, leave it where it is.
- ✓ If you get a piece of an inedible item, such as a stem or bone, politely remove it from your mouth with a utensil and place it on the edge of your plate trying to cover with another piece of food.
- ✓ If encountering something un-chewable or undesirable, hold your napkin up to your mouth and discreetly dispose of it. Place your

napkin on the side and quietly ask your waiter for a new one. An alternative is to politely excuse yourself to the restroom while keeping it in your mouth, and dispose of it there.

- ✓ Toothpicks should be used discreetly and in private; not at the table. A good idea is to go to the restroom after dining to check your teeth and freshen up.
- ✓ Never season your food before trying it. Do not complain about the quality of your food or small errors. If you dislike an item in the meal, move food around on the plate a little to appear as though you at least tried it. If you have a food allergy, it is your (the guest's) responsibility to notify the host ahead of time.
- ✓ When sharing a plate of chips or veggies with a dip or sauce with others, apply the "Single Dip Rule" - that is, dip only once; do not insert a food item you have taken a bite from back into a shared bowl of dip or sauce
- ✓ Do not spit into your napkin. Do not blow on your food. If food is too hot to eat, let it sit until it cools.
- ✓ If someone decides to claim your bread plate, let it go. It is NEVER good manners to point out someone else's lack of manners.
- ✓ Do not use lipstick, makeup, floss, combs, or toothpicks at the table.
- ✓ Do not push plates away or stack empty plates when finished.
- ✓ Never ask for a doggy bag.
- ✓ Be polite to serving staff, make eye contact and say "excuse me" to get their attention as needed, and "please and thank you"

✓ When you are at a meal interview, you may feel pressured to talk so much you don't get a chance to eat your food. You should not solve this problem by talking with your mouth full. Instead, come to the interview armed with some questions to ask the interviewer. This will allow you to eat while listening to their answers and also shows that you have done your homework!

Passing Food Etiquette
✓ Plates are served on the left and removed from your right.
✓ Do not reach across the table for an item, but politely ask the person next to you to pass. Pass "community food" such as the breadbasket, salt and pepper, and salad dressing to the right- the point being that the food is to be moving in only one direction.
✓ The person closest to the plate should offer to the person on the left, serve themselves, and then pass the food to the right.
✓ Do not serve yourself first when asked to pass something. Always pass to the right, and always include the service plate. It is considered rude to use it first before passing it to the person who asked for it.
✓ When passing items such as a creamer, syrup pitcher, or gravy boat, always pass it with the handle pointing toward the recipient.
✓ Set any passed item directly on the table instead of passing hand-to-hand. Once using or taking from a passed item, set it in a "central" location easily accessible by others if possible -do not keep it close to you.

✓ Never use your own utensils to serve food out of a communal dish.
✓ One diner either holds the dish as the next diner takes some food, or he hands it to the person, who then serves himself.
✓ If a platter for sharing is present it is passed around the table, with each diner holding it as the person next to him serves himself, using only the serving utensils provided.
✓ Any heavy or awkward dishes are put on the table with each pass.

Bread Passing Etiquette (More on this covered in previous chapter too)
✓ If the loaf is not cut, cut a few pieces, offer them to the person to your left, and then pass the basket to your right.
✓ Do not touch the loaf with your fingers- instead use the cloth in the bread basket as a buffer to steady the bread as you slice it.
✓ Place the bread and butter on your butter plate- yours being on your left- then break off a bite sized piece of bread, put a little butter on it, and eat it.

Salt and Pepper Etiquette
✓ Always taste before salting. Be sure to taste the food before putting salt or pepper on it.
✓ Always pass salt and pepper together. If a person asks for just one, pass both anyway.
✓ Saltcellars. Some hosts prefer to use saltcellars, which salt shakers have largely replaced. If there is no spoon in the saltcellar, use the tip of a clean knife to take some salt. If the saltcellar is for you alone, you may either

use the tip of your knife or you may take a pinch with your fingers. If it is to be shared with others, never use your fingers or a knife that is not clean.

✓ Salt you have taken from the cellar should be put on the bread-and-butter plate or on the rim of whatever plate is before you.

A Quick-At-Glance Table Manners-Do's and Don'ts

Before you commence your Meal

✓ Eat something an hour before the meal, if possible, to maintain focus on the conversation, and not the food.

✓ If you have allergies or food restrictions and if you know in advance the restaurant where you will be dining, look up the menu and make a list of possible foods that will not hinder your allergy or dietary restrictions.

✓ If you are the host, you should always try to arrive at the restaurant before your guests. You may wait for your guests in the foyer of the restaurant or at your table, but if you choose to wait at your table, give the maitre d' a description of your guests and ask him to direct them to your table.

✓ When approaching the table in a restaurant, if the maitre d' leads the group to the table, the guests should follow the maitre d' and the host should follow the guests. If the maitre d' does not lead the group, the host should lead.

✓ If you are the host, and if there is a guest that is late, rather than delay dinner for everyone to accommodate the arrival of the late guest, dinner is held no longer than 15 to 20 minutes.

✓ If one or more guests are ten minutes late, ask the maitre d' to seat the group and show the other guests to the table upon their arrival. Once seated, the punctual guests can order drinks and examine the menu. After waiting 15 or 20 minutes, the group should order their meals.

- ✓ At an informal dinner, the guests enter the dining room in whatever order is convenient. When seating arrangements are not designated by place cards, usually the hostess enters the dining room first to tell everyone where to sit.
- ✓ When the guest of honor is a high-ranking female dignitary, such as the President of a country, she enters the dining room first with the host. The dignitary's husband follows with the hostess. If the guest of honor is a high-ranking male dignitary, he enters the dining room first with the hostess. The host enters the dining room second with the dignitary's wife.
- ✓ Place cards identify the places people are to sit; they are used to eliminate confusion when more than six people dine together. At formal affairs, which usually involve a large group, individual places are always designated by place cards.
- ✓ Your cell phone or other personal electronics should not be part of the dining experience. Either keep on silent your personal devises or power them off for the duration of the event and keep them put away. Checking your phone at the table implies that you have something more important going on than conversing with or listening to your hosts and is considered rude
- ✓ The place of honor is to the right side of the host because most people are right-handed.

- ✓ Smoking of cigarettes must never happen at the table. Smoking is offensive to nonsmokers and affects the palate.
- ✓ Always follow your host's lead: when to sit, how much to order, how fast/slow to eat, what to discuss, and if/when to take off a suit jacket.
- ✓ It is not proper table manners to keep a hat on when eating. However, wearing any type hat is becoming more acceptable in fast food restaurants and in casual settings.
- ✓ As a guest, if you know a maid or a butler, rather than draw attention to the fact and interrupt conversation, give a brief greeting, such as "Nice to see you."
- ✓ If at a job interview, follow the host's lead when ordering food or drink and avoid sloppy or difficult-to-eat dishes. Do not participate in unpleasant or controversial topics of conversation.
- ✓ Seeing the room layout gives you a clue on how to proceed at the reception. If no tables are available, you should only have a drink or your food in your hand - never both.
- ✓ You should be prepared to greet and shake hands with individuals. If having a drink hold it in your left hand to keep your right hand dry and ready to shake hands. If eating hold your plate on the right hand and eat with the left hand. When someone approaches, you are able to switch the plate to your left hand and your right hand is clean and ready to shake.
- ✓ Always be ready to stand and greet people. Networking and/or mingling are an important aspect of a business function, even if the event is described as a social gathering.

- ✓ Be sure to greet or introduce yourself to the host/hostess.
- ✓ Focus eye contact on that individual and after sometime, politely excuse yourself to move on to someone else.

During the Meal

- ✓ Be generous with "please," "thank you," and "excuse me," especially with the wait staff
- ✓ Turn off or silence all electronic devices before entering the restaurant. If you forgot to turn off your cell phone, and it rings, immediately turn it off. Do not answer the call. Do not text and do not browse the net at the table. It is bad manners
- ✓ A purse on the table crowds and disturbs the setting of the table; therefore in a restaurant or public place, it is held on the lap or placed close at hand. But in a private residence it is left wherever the hostess suggests, such as in a bedroom or on a chair.
- ✓ At a banquet, eating commences as soon as those on either side of you are served. However, at a meal served buffet style, begin eating when you are ready.
- ✓ At a restaurant buffet, never go back to the buffet for a refill with a dirty plate. Leave it for the waitperson to pick up and start afresh with a clean plate.
- ✓ At some top posh restaurants, steamed hand towels are brought to diners at the end of the meal. Use the towel to wipe your hands and, if necessary, the area around your mouth. (Wiping the back of your neck or behind your ears is best not done in a restaurant.) Most

waiters will take the towel away as soon as you've finished. If not, leave the towel at the left of your plate, on top of your loosely folded napkin.

✓ Place your napkin in your lap immediately upon sitting down. Unfold it while it is in your lap.

✓ Do not hunch your shoulders over your plate. Likewise, slouching back in your chair may indicate that you are not interested in the meal

✓ To show you are ready to order, close your menu and place it on the table.

✓ Order appetizers, dessert and alcohol only if your host suggests (Limit to one alcoholic beverage to stay sharp)

✓ Don't order the most expensive items on the menu. If you aren't sure which price range to adhere to, follow the lead of the host.

✓ Avoid messy foods, such as spaghetti and ribs. It is best not to order finger foods or anything with bones

✓ Do not change your order once it is made, and never send the food back.

✓ Use the "outside-in" rule to guide you into which knife, fork, or spoon to use at the dinner table. Use utensils on the outside first and work your way in with each new course.

✓ The "no elbows on the table" rule applies only when you are actually eating. When no utensils are being used, putting your elbows on the table is ok.

✓ A cocktail glass is not brought to the dinner table because water and several wines are served with a multi-course meal. Leave the cocktail glass in the room where cocktails are taken.

- ✓ Go for simple foods, such as meat, simple salad, and soup. Avoid spaghetti, pizza, and hand-held items. If it is a fixed menu, and you do not like what you are being served, remain gracious and do not refuse the food.
- ✓ If your dish is not what you ordered, or if it isn't cooked to order, or it tastes spoiled, or if you discover a hair or a pest in the dish, then sending the dish back is entirely appropriate. But you should discreetly inform the waiter of the situation and ask for a replacement.
- ✓ If you are served food that you cannot eat, eat what you can and leave the rest on your plate.
- ✓ If you are unfamiliar about how to eat a particular food item, you can do any of these: (1) Wait until the host starts to eat and follow suit. (2) You can ask how the food should be eaten (fingers or fork, for example). (3) You can avoid the food altogether.
- ✓ When asked to pass the salt, pass both the salt and pepper.
- ✓ Never add any seasoning to your food, without you first tasting your food. It is bad manners
- ✓ At a restaurant, the waiter serves food from your left and beverages from your right side.
- ✓ As the waiter offers you a platter, help yourself with the serving fork in your left hand and the serving spoon in your right.
- ✓ If soup is too hot, stir it, don't blow.
- ✓ When eating soup, always, spoon the soup away from you towards the center of the soup bowl.

- ✓ Crackers are not to be put in your soup during a formal meal.
- ✓ Start the bread by offering it to the left before helping yourself. Then pass it to the right.
- ✓ When holding a utensil, rest your other hand in your lap. When not holding any utensils, both hands remain in the lap. Do not fidget, and always keep your hands away from your hair.
- ✓ Food served on a plate is eaten with a fork, and food served in a bowl is taken with a spoon. When two eating utensils or two serving utensils are presented together, such as a fork and spoon, the fork is used to steady the portion, and the spoon to cut and convey the bite to the mouth.
- ✓ When a platter contains a combination of foods, take a moderate serving of each, including the garnish. If a course is presented that contains another food underneath, such as toast or lettuce, take the entire portion. As a courtesy to the last guest, make sure to leave enough food on the platter so he or she has a choice from several portions. Take the portion nearest to you.
- ✓ When served a half chicken, use your knife and fork to cut the wing and leg away from the breast before you start eating any of the meat.
- ✓ It is acceptable to eat your chicken with your fingers on three occasions: a picnic, at home, or if it is served in a basket.
- ✓ In a restaurant, if a soiled utensil is laid on the table, ask the waiter for a clean one. But in a private residence, rather than embarrass the

hostess by wiping a soiled utensil clean, bear up in silence.

✓ At an informal meal, the guests assist with service by passing the dishes nearest to them. To avoid congestion, food is passed to the right.

✓ For items on the table that are out of your reach, don't lean past the person sitting next to you

✓ When a serving bowl is passed upon request, say "Thank you." But when you have to refuse a service, a verbal rejection of "No, thank you," is provided.

✓ Cut your food into only one or two bite-sized pieces at a time. Do not cut all your meat at once; this is reserved for children only.

✓ When finger food is taken from a tray, place it on a plate. Don't lick your fingers; use a napkin.

✓ Do not speak while eating. Finish what is in your mouth, rest your fork on your plate and then speak.

✓ To prevent traces of food from your appearing on the rim of the vessel, like a drinking water glass, make sure the mouth is free of food and blot the lips with a napkin before taking a sip of a beverage.

✓ When tasting another person's food, you can either hand your fork to the person, who can spear a bite-sized piece from their plate and hand the fork back to you, or (if the person is sitting close by) hold your plate toward the person so that he/she can put a small portion on the edge.

- ✓ Always do one thing at a time at the table. If you want to sip your wine, temporarily rest your fork or knife on the plate, and then get into sipping.
- ✓ If you spill food, discreetly retrieve it with your knife or fork and place it at the side of your plate. You may also discreetly dip your napkin into your water glass and wipe a small spill from your clothing. If food falls on the floor, leave it. If it falls on the table and is a big piece, use your fork and move it to a corner of your plate
- ✓ Never leave your spoon in your cup, soup bowl, or stemmed glass. Rest the spoon on the saucer or soup plate between bites or when finished.
- ✓ Always, eat slowly, by enjoying it, as this also encourages conversation
- ✓ Eating and making a noise, like scraping a plate, loudly chewing, smacking and slurping food can be unpleasant and impolite and are bad table manners.
- ✓ Food caught between the teeth can be annoying or uncomfortable, so wait to remove it in private.
- ✓ White wine glasses are held by the stem, not the bowl. Red wine glasses may be held by the bowl.
- ✓ Asking for a second helping is not proper table manners at a formal dinner but is permissible at an informal one.
- ✓ Never hold your glass up for a refill.
- ✓ Food is removed from the mouth in the manner in which it was put into the mouth.

Food put into the mouth with a utensil is removed with a utensil.

✓ You can take up extra gravy or sauce only with a piece of bread on the end of a fork; the soaked bread is then brought to the mouth with the fork.

✓ You may not use a toothpick in public to dislodge debris from in between your teeth - not at the table, not on your way out of the restaurant; hanging the toothpick out of your mouth...only at home when you are alone in total darkness

✓ If you notice a speck of food on someone's face, you're doing them a favor by subtly calling attention to it. You might signal silently by using your index finger to lightly tap whatever part of the face is affected.

✓ If you drop a utensil, pick it up yourself if you can and let the waiter know you need a new one. If you cannot reach it, inform the waiter and ask for a replacement.

✓ If sugar, crackers, cream, or other accompaniments to meals are served with paper wrappers or in plastic or cardboard containers, the wrappers should be crumpled up tightly and either tucked under the rim of your plate or placed on the edge of the saucer or butter plate.

✓ If food is spilled on another guest, apologize and offer to pay for cleaning (but let the other person wipe up the soiled garment).

✓ Never gesture with a knife or fork in your hands.

✓ The water is for sipping, not for washing down your food. So do not gargle at the table.

- ✓ When sneezing or coughing at the table is unavoidable, cover your nose or mouth with a napkin and proceed as quietly as possible. Turn your head away from the table and cover your mouth. Don't clear your throat loudly. Except in an emergency, don't use a napkin to blow your nose. Leave the table and use a handkerchief instead.
- ✓ When a burp is coming out, cover the mouth with a napkin, quietly burp, and say, "Excuse me." For an attack of hiccups, excuse yourself from the table until they have passed.
- ✓ When using a finger bowl, dip your fingers into the water and then dry them with your napkin.
- ✓ Chewing ice at the table or spitting it back in the glass is not acceptable adult business behavior.
- ✓ When coffee or tea is placed on the table without first having been poured by the waiter, the person nearest the pot should offer to pour, filling his or her own cup last.
- ✓ If you do not wish to drink coffee or tea, simply leave your cup turned down
- ✓ When leaving for the restroom, simply say "excuse me, please; I'll be right back" Leaving without a word is rude.
- ✓ As a guest, a compliment on the cuisine is always appreciated.
- ✓ Don't photograph your food.

After the Meal
- ✓ The host will signal the end of the meal by placing his/her napkin on the table.
- ✓ If you are the host, inform in advance, the waiter or maitre d' that you are to receive the

bill. Once the meal is finished, ask the waiter for the bill. If there is no established host at a business lunch or dinner, the most senior professional is generally responsible for the bill.

✓ Put used tissue/napkin in your pocket or purse - don't leave it on the table for others to be forced to view, or in your chair for a server to remove.

✓ It is acceptable table manners to take leftover food home from a restaurant, except if on a date or business lunch or dinner.

✓ Remember to thank your host. A thank you note is recommended!

Dining Conversations

You have very little time to make a good first impression. We had seen in an earlier chapter on how to handle that first 30 seconds, the social ritual part- shaking hands and introducing yourself. Now you must build on that first impression- you have to make that person feel good about being with you, even for a brief encounter.

According to studies, 75% of us feel awkward and shy when we meet new people and find it difficult to start a conversation with a stranger. People are afraid of being rejected, or saying the wrong thing or just not fitting into the group.

Here are a few thoughts for ensuring the right conversations at Lunches/ Dinners

- ✓ Reflect on why you are there. Consider the purpose/context of the dining experience. Is it part of a job interview process? A formal or informal gathering of co-workers? A business deal? A major project or sale? A partnership deal?
- ✓ Come prepared accordingly: Remember that business dining is all about conversation. So come prepared with appropriate dinner conversation. You need to contribute to your table talk in a way that sets other dinner guests at ease. So do all your research in advance. Who will be attending? What interests might they have? What topics are in line with the focus of the function? When the inevitable lapse in conversation occurs, know leading questions that will encourage table

guests to begin talking about themselves. Questions or statements such as: "I'm interested in knowing a little about the kind of work you do." "Please tell me about your interest in the organization represented here." "Have you heard the speaker before?"

✓ Be well informed
- What are the current events for today? Do you have small talk options ready for the function, if needed?
- Read at least one daily newspaper and a weekly news magazine
- Before going to an event, read the headlines of the day. Current events are perfect for small talk. And don't forget the sports and arts pages.
- Bring up these topics during the first conversational lull; the other person will be grateful for your filling the silence and will most likely follow your lead.

✓ Be Curious: It's not about you. Try focusing more on the other person.

✓ Wait for the host to initiate a discussion: Generally, the host initiates the business discussion. Business, if not urgent, is often discussed toward the end of the meal or over coffee. If you are the host, it's your job to steer the conversation, to suggest topics for discussion, and to make sure that everyone at the table is given the opportunity to be part of the general conversation. When the table isn't involved in a general discussion, be a good conversationalist with the people seated on either side of you.

- ✓ Pay attention to the thread of conversation and participate when appropriate. Don't interrupt or repeatedly turn the topic of conversation to you or your interests.
- ✓ Take a glance at the person to see if there is anything about them that could start a conversation. People will be flattered by and appreciate your interest in them.
- ✓ If you're at a concert, trade meet- talk about the group, the room, food, entertainment. The same goes for wherever you may be.
- ✓ Try to choose universal topics of conversation in which all may have an interest. If you can't think of anything to say, then just listen attentively, and ask questions to generate conversation.
- ✓ Ask them appropriate, relevant questions about themselves-to start the conversation. Listen actively and show appreciation as they speak. Your conversation partner feels important when you ask questions; people like to talk about themselves, so let them do it.
- ✓ When you ask questions, there is a lot less pressure for your partner- you are perceived as caring, open and humble. Be a good listener! Ask OPEN ENDED questions that lead to longer answers. These types of questions usually ask who, what, when, where, why, and how, and use verbs that deal with your senses. (Covered separately under a different chapter)

  What do you think of...?
  How do you know so and so...?
  What got you into...?
  What gave you the idea...?

Describe….tell me about.

It's a good idea to prepare some questions before you go to an event. That way you'll have something to fall back on.

✓ Now share brief, reflective relevant comments about yourself if asked.
✓ Have only one conversation at a time
✓ Don't dominate the table. Give everyone a fair share to speak. And remember that you are responsible for conversing with your "triangle."

Conversing with your "Triangle"

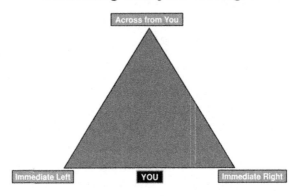

✓ Pay attention to people's physical needs. Do they need another drink? Something more on their plate?
✓ Avoid a loud tone of voice. Do not use profanities. Be sensitive to others before initiating conversation on topics that may not be suitable- avoid anything of a vulgar, graphic, or otherwise unpleasant nature. Ensure the conversation is entirely free of controversial subjects-Never tell jokes, as you never know who you could offend.

✓ If you are someone else's guest, even if part of a group, don't criticize the food, restaurant, etc. - this can cause embarrassment on the part of the "host."

Starting a conversation

A good place to start is to think of common interests.
For starting a conversation or breaking the ice with strangers, think of: F.O.R.M.

F-Family
O-Occupation
R-Recreation
M-Money (economy)

Small talk can be a real saver in many situations. It fills the voids in conversations, helps ease tense moments, sets others at ease, and helps one become acquainted with others. There are two ways to make initiating small talk a little easier.

✓ The first is to be well-informed. To be able to discuss topics such as current best-selling books, news events, famous people, fitness crazes, technological advances, travel, and sports. These are all appropriate small talk subjects.

✓ The second way to ease into small talk is by asking others about themselves, their family, work, or hobby.

Here are some topics that are appropriate to speak up and get you started:

Small Talk Topics

✓ Your location or venue
✓ Shows, movies, plays, etc
✓ Art
✓ Food, restaurants, or cooking
✓ Their hobbies

- ✓ Their professional interests and responsibilities
- ✓ Sports
- ✓ The climate
- ✓ Travel
- ✓ Their local shopping favorites

Good Topics

- ✓ Current events, news etc
- ✓ Emerging Trends, Best Practices (Eg. How's business been amidst recession/ challenge etc?)
- ✓ Career Journeys + Performance/Burn Out Advice
- ✓ Food
- ✓ Memberships
- ✓ Mutual friends
- ✓ Hobbies
- ✓ Industry talk
- ✓ Styles/ Trends
- ✓ Sports

Bad Topics

- ✓ Any personal issues such as: family, health/ illnesses/ divorces/ separation/ affairs etc which may trigger something
- ✓ Religion/ religious beliefs
- ✓ Politics
- ✓ Salaries/ financial situation
- ✓ The cost of things
- ✓ Off color jokes- Racial, ethnic, and sexually oriented jokes
- ✓ Gossip
- ✓ Weight, height, shoe size, age or mental health

Here are some ways of opening a conversation for various situations:

For Prospects/ Customers:

- ✓ What were some of the key initiatives you took that brought you this far?
- ✓ What makes you stand out from your competitor?
- ✓ What's the most exciting thing about your business?
- ✓ What's the most exciting thing about your team?
- ✓ What are some of the most significant changes in your industry in recent years?
- ✓ If you could go back one year in time, what would you do differently?
- ✓ I'm honestly curious to know your story
- ✓ Tell me about your...?
- ✓ What's your company's biggest priority right now?
- ✓ How has business changed since we talked last?
- ✓ How are your efforts in [related business area]?
- ✓ What can I do to help you achieve....?

Common event

- ✓ What do you think of the conference so far? ... How have the sessions been? What did you particularly like?
- ✓ What inspired you to become a member of this body?

Company/Job

- ✓ Tom mentioned of how you were recently given additional responsibilities...Congratulations!

- ✓ How do you like this new role? What are some of the new areas responsibilities now? How different is it to what you were doing?

Business/Industry
- ✓ Off what I know, you were all along into production? How and what made you get into this active sales role?
- ✓ How have the recent changes in the government regulations affecting your business?

Location
- ✓ I live in Delhi. Where are you from?
- ✓ This is my very first visit to Mauritius. What do you recommend I see while I'm here?
- ✓ What is it that you like about living in Colombo?

Sports
- ✓ I hear that your favorite past time is playing golf. Did you see the xxxx Cup this year?
- ✓ Last night's cricket match kept me in real suspense. What did you feel about it?

Travel
- ✓ Sarah was mentioning that you just returned from Turkey. How was your trip?
- ✓ I know you'd been to Israel recently. Our family is also planning a trip sometime next year. How do you recommend we go about this?

Hobbies/Interests
- ✓ I noticed that you volunteered in the company's cancer prevention drive? That's certainly a good deed to do. How did the event go?
- ✓ What are your hobbies or interests outside of work?

Some Common Conversation Killers

How do you know if a question is too personal? Ask yourself how you would feel if someone asked you the question and everybody in the room could hear the answer. If you'd feel comfortable, the question is OK.

Avoid:
- ✓ Bragging
- ✓ Interrupting
- ✓ Monopolizing
- ✓ Not playing the game

If someone asks a question, give him or her something to work with. Don't do this: "How was your vacation?' "Fine"

Instead: "How was your vacation?" "Fine The beach was great and we went boating every day."

With your Boss
When you are out with your boss for lunch or dinner...

Here are a few points you can keep in mind while on a dinner/lunch with your boss.
- ✓ Focus on your attire-Dress Professionally
- ✓ Be punctual and on time
- ✓ Be active and enthusiastic all the time
- ✓ Watch your body language and mannerisms
- ✓ Maintain a presence of mind and positive attitude
- ✓ Let your host take the lead
- ✓ Stay focused
- ✓ Pick appropriate topics- do some groundwork, know what to talk about
- ✓ Matchup to the audience at food and drinks
- ✓ Express your gratitude

Things to talk while having lunch or dinner with your boss:
- ✓ Sports
- ✓ Music
- ✓ Literature: depending on his/her age
- ✓ Office history: their years of experience, his/her climb up, his/her challenges
- ✓ Assignments/ Projects
- ✓ Food
- ✓ Hobbies

Few things which your boss may want to hear from you
- ✓ Things you enjoy doing
- ✓ Things you find boring
- ✓ About your knowledge gaps
- ✓ Feedback and goals
- ✓ New innovative methods to implement
- ✓ How your life has been influenced by the company
- ✓ Career progression

Things to avoid talking while having lunch with your boss:
- ✓ Don't get too personal:
- ✓ Strictly avoid prejudiced topics
- ✓ Do not blabber/ blurt out others mistakes
- ✓ Be careful about your remarks: Think of the repercussions before you speak
- ✓ Do not whine or complain
- ✓ Never talk office politics/ gossip
- ✓ Toilet humor
- ✓ Indiscretions: You cross your limit and lose the impression in front of the boss

Drinks and Wine Etiquette

Restaurants are happy to provide complimentary tastes of wine because they know that it will make you more comfortable ordering a glass. It's okay to ask for a taste of wines offered by the glass, since those wine bottles are already opened. However, if you plan to order a bottle from the wine list, you'll need to proceed without the benefit of a sample.

When the wine steward brings the bottle, check the label to be sure it is the exact wine that was ordered. Feel the cork after the wine is opened. Check for moistness, which is one way to determine whether or not the wine has been properly stored. A cork that is too dry or damaged will let air into the bottle and damage the wine. Smell the cork to make sure there is no unpleasant odor. A hint of vinegar will indicate the wine has gone bad. Most restaurants offer a smaller selection of wines by the glass. When ordering wine by the glass, you should be aware that you may be getting wine from a previously opened bottle. You may want to ask the server when the bottle was opened. If it has been opened for one or more days, you may want to make another selection.

The first taste is offered to the host/hostess, who will take a sip and indicate approval or disapproval. The host/hostess is served last, after all the guests have been served.

If the host and/or others at the table order a glass of wine, you may do so if you wish. Formal dinners can serve a different wine with each course, and you do not have to finish each glass.

How to Order Wine? If you are unsure what to order, look at the menu and ask the waiter for a recommendation. Start by selecting a wine in the category you are interested in and find a wine at the price point you are comfortable with. Show the sommelier/ steward your selection and ask for his opinion, but place your finger on the price, rather than the name.

A good rule of thumb to determine how many bottles to order is to start with a half bottle per person. If the group includes at least three people, you may try ordering a bottle of red and a bottle of white.

The order of the wine glasses begins with the one closest to you:

- ✓ Sherry (Soup course)
- ✓ White wine is usually served with poultry and fish)
- ✓ Red wine is with the Meat course and usually preferred for dark meats and red meats and sauces
- ✓ Water goblet

How do you hold the wine glasses?

If you are drinking white wine, hold the glass by the stem.

If it is red wine, hold the glass by the bottom of the goblet

The reasons are practical. White wine is served more chilled than red, so holding the glass by the stem helps it to remain chilled. Red wine is served warmer than white, therefore the heat of your hand around the goblet will not diminish the wine's bouquet.

Hold your drink in your left hand to keep your right hand dry and ready to shake hands.

It is perfectly fine to refrain from alcoholic drinks

Never turn your wine glass over to indicate you do not want to drink. Simply use your hand on the glass to show that you are not interested. Whether you drink or not is a personal choice and you are not bound to give long-winded excuses as a reply. So do not make it sound as if drinking alcohol is a crime.

Simply thank the host for offering the drink and state your preference. S/he would be glad to get you the drink of your choice.

One glass of wine may be acceptable.

Toasting Etiquette

Toasting to love, friendship, health, wealth and happiness has been practiced by almost every culture from the beginning of recorded history. Traditionally, the host or hostess offers the first toast. Around a table with friends, however, a guest can propose the first toast (and often does), usually as a way to thank the host for bringing everyone together. At a wedding however, it is usually the best man that leads the toasting at a wedding reception.

Unless your toast has been designated as the key one of the evening, think of K.I.S.S.- Keep it Short and Sweet or you can also think of 3 B's- Begin Right, Be Brief and Be Seated. The key toast is a small speech of sorts, and it should be composed in writing and rehearsed by the speaker well in advance.

The host always toasts first. Gain the crowd's attention by standing and raising your glass; banging on a glass with a knife should be considered a measure of last resort. Gentle is better than hearty when it comes to clinking. You don't want to be remembered as the one who smashed the glass and bathed everyone around you in red wine.

Make sure that all glasses are filled before toasting, and ensure that everyone is involved. Nothing is more uncomfortable than standing up in front of a room full of friends or strangers to propose a toast while having your request largely ignored, with all of them busy in their own groups. Instead, enlist the help of your colleagues and friends by asking them to assist in quieting their respective groups when they see you stand with your glass raised. At formal occasions the person toasting stands, along with the others toasting, while the person being toasted remains seated.

There are many occasions where a toast is appropriate like weddings, anniversaries, christenings, Christmas and New Year parties, birthdays, reunions, retirements or for the birth of a child. If you know the occasion, you should prepare your toast in advance. Write it down, keep it brief and practice until you feel confident. Be sure to speak slowly and loud enough for all guests to hear.

Hold the glass up towards the center of the table, raising it only to eye level, ensuring you have eye contact with the person across from you.

If it is an informal party such as an example of a Christmas night, the host might just say something like this, "Thank you for coming and I'm delighted we are all here on this cozy Christmas night, as we get ready to welcome the New Year ahead of us. Here's to a glorious 2023."

The guests respond by taking a sip of their drinks - but never emptying the glass. A person who doesn't drink alcohol should join in as well, toasting with a soft drink or even water.

The person being toasted does not drink to himself. The best bet here is to do nothing except look humble and appreciative. Then after everyone has toasted, the person being toasted to, rises and initiates a return toast by saying a simple thanks and taking a sip. He may also raise his own glass to propose a toast to the host, or anyone else he sees fit to honor. It is no small feat to pull off a successful event, and honoring your host with a toast is a nice way to show your gratitude. Say something like, "Thank you for including all of us in such a fun and festive Christmas party. You went out of your way to make this night so special and your hard work has certainly paid off. Here's to Jonathan, a lovely and gracious host."

When in an informal gathering with glasses are raised it can just be with shouts of "Cheers!", "To your health and joy!" or "To Cindy and Bob!" Including a few personal remarks, praise, or a relevant story or joke –can be a good idea, provided the same is clean and in line with the event or occasion. Ideally, a good toast is one that is centered around the occasion or gathering and using a concluding phrase such as "Here's to?" or "Cheers."

At private or small informal dinners, it is acceptable for everyone-the one toasting, and the one being toasted included to remain seated.

Never refuse to participate; you can always use an empty glass or non-alcoholic beverage. The glasses don't have to hold wine like the others; non-drinkers can toast with water, juice, or a soft drink.

Tea Etiquette

The general time for tea is four o'clock in the afternoon, with service running sometimes from two to five o'clock. For this reason they are called "afternoon tea" or simply "tea" and not to be called "high tea", as it's not the same thing.

These afternoon teas are social events that can happen when you have to entertain a visiting friend, celebrate a special occasion, a house warming party and a wonderful way to spend time with friends. It is far less formal today, but some simple rules of etiquette still apply.

The tea session is made up of three courses of food with a pot of tea in the following order:

1. The savory course with finger sandwiches
2. The scones course served with clotted cream and jam
3. Sweet cakes pastries

Tea equipment and flatware

The standard china tea set consists of:

1. A teapot,
2. A creamer for the milk,
3. A sugar bowl,
4. A pitcher of hot water (for those who prefer weak tea), and
5. A plate for lemon slices.

Depending on the number of guests, the teacups, saucers and spoons are placed on the right side, while the flatware (for serving cakes, pastries, bread etc), plates, knives and butter spreaders and tea napkins are placed on the left. If there are dishes with jam and cream where everyone takes a portion, then each dish should have its own serving spoon. Never use your own utensils to dip into the jam or cream dish.

However, when seated at a table in a private home or in a tea-room, there should be at each place setting the following:

- ✓ A knife or butter spreader on the right side of the plate
- ✓ A fork on the left side.
- ✓ A teaspoon may be placed on the saucer holding the cup or to the right of the knife.

Here are some important Do's and Don'ts as you begin:

- ✓ The dress code these days is "smart casual". Suits and fancy dresses are not necessary. However, it may differ depending on the venue, so always be sure to check before attending.
- ✓ It is required that the host assigns one guest to pour tea for everyone at the table.
- ✓ Never serve yourself first (if you're the host!) or overfill the teacups.
- ✓ The assigned pourer will pour tea into an empty tea cup. Use a tea strainer if needed and fill the teacups up to three quarters of the way.
- ✓ Never add milk before adding tea to a tea cup, as not every guest drinks tea with milk, and adding the tea first gives the drinker the option of adding milk or not. You want to make sure to leave room to allow your guests to add milk, lemon or sweetener to their tea if desired.
- ✓ When you sit down instantly drape the napkin on your lap with the crease facing towards you. This will save you from any unsightly

spills and show that you're well versed in the art of dining etiquette.

✓ Stir the tea with a teaspoon up and down (6 o'clock to 12 o'clock motion) gently and noiselessly by moving 2-3 times without touching the sides of the teacup. Then set the teaspoon on the saucer behind the cup, with the handle of the spoon pointing in the same direction as the handle of the cup in a four O'clock position similar to a clock.

✓ Never leave a spoon upright in the cup, or place the spoon on the saucer in front of the cup or let the spoon drop, after stirring the tea, with a clank onto the saucer.

✓ When holding the teacup, it is done by meeting your thumb and index finger in the handle and resting your middle finger under it.

✓ Never hook your finger through the handle or stick your pinky out. That's a common mistake as most assume it's being fancy. But, pinkies out is not acceptable. When holding the teacup keep the pinkie down!

✓ The saucer stays on the table. Don't hold it in your hands while enjoying tea. You only hold your saucer and tea cup together if you are standing or sitting with no table in front of you.

✓ Don't wrap your hands around the cup.

✓ Wait for the tea to cool. Whilst blowing on hot tea might seem like the practical thing to do, this is actually considered bad manners in the world of afternoon tea.

✓ You may begin to eat the savories and tea sandwiches first, followed by the scones and then the sweets. You can use your fingers too as after all, afternoon tea is all finger foods!

- ✓ Break the scone in half by hand and eat each half separately or enjoy by breaking off bite-sized chunks. Spread cream first then top with jam.
- ✓ Do not use cutlery or be tempted to eat the sweet course first.
- ✓ At the end of the tea, the napkin is not refolded but picked up by the center and placed loosely to the left of the plate with the open edge to the right.
- ✓ Enjoy Yourself! Most importantly whilst following the rules of etiquette is important don't let yourself get so focused on them that you forget to enjoy the experience!

Tipping Etiquette

Note: (*As this book is addressed to an international audience, the tipping amounts are very general just to provide an idea. It is important to do your groundwork before you travel anywhere*)

Tipping is very important, yet it can be super confusing, as there is no true standard for tipping. When, who and how much to tip can depend on any number of factors, including the specific situation, service, or even the location. Tipping however, is all about showing appreciation for good service. Standard tipping amounts on average usually range from 5% to 20%, with anything above 20% indicating excellent service, but this definitely does vary with the service provider, service received, culture and country

Here are some general guidelines:
- ✓ Tip on the pre-tax amount of the bill, not on the total.
- ✓ Do not make a show of the amount being tipped. It must be done discreetly.
- ✓ The usual tip internationally, is ten (10) to twenty (20) percent on the pre-tax amount of the bill
- ✓ Sometimes a gratuity is already included in the bill. But if you think it is deserved, you can leave an additional amount.
- ✓ Sometimes a restaurant may have a 'no-tipping' policy. In such cases, you may want to leave a note of appreciation, or ask to see a

manager and share what you loved most about the server
- ✓ Not every country has a culture of tipping- So keep in mind that tipping etiquette can change depending on country/ culture. If the service is bad, you don't have to tip, when you're not satisfied with the service.
- ✓ If the service is good, being generous can help with even better service in future.
- ✓ There is no need to tip the owner or proprietor of the restaurant, even if he or she serves you.
- ✓ You also do not need to tip the maitre d' unless they have done a special favor or arranged a special meal for you.

Here are some general Tipping Percentages
- ✓ Self-service restaurants/ Buffet: 5-10%
- ✓ Extra accommodating waiters: a few additional bucks for extra special service
- ✓ Waiter (serving at tables):15-20% pre-tax
- ✓ Lingering at your table on a busy night: an extra: 10 to 15%
- ✓ Waiter (buffet): 10%
- ✓ Bartender: 15-20%
- ✓ Host or Maitre d': Not necessary just for greeting you and showing you to your table. But a small amount for going above and beyond to find you a table on a busy night or on occasion, if you are a regular patron
- ✓ Tip for Delivery: 10-15% of the bill depending on the size of the order and difficulty of delivery
- ✓ Massage therapists: 15% to 20%,
- ✓ Hairdressers or nail technicians: 10% to 20%

- ✓ Restroom Attendant- depending on the level of service
- ✓ Valet: Tip when the car is returned to you.
- ✓ Uber driver: 15% to 20% of the fare for taxi services
- ✓ Musicians
- In some posh restaurants with piano/ musical instrument entertainment, you do not tip the musician unless there is tip jar.
- If you have made song requests, tip them and do so for each song.
- You needn't stop eating when musicians perform table side. Just smile and thank them as you tip when the musicians finish.

Settling the Bill

As a Guest:
If you are someone's guest at a meal, ask the person what he/she recommends. By doing this, you will learn price range guidelines and have an idea of what to order. Usually order an item in the mid price range. Also keep in mind, the person who typically initiates the meal will pay. The person who does the inviting does the paying. If someone invites you to lunch and the server places the bill on the table, don't make a grab for it if you are a guest. Let the person who invited you have the opportunity to pick up the bill and deal with it. If being treated by someone, always thank them

As the Host:
If you are the host, tell the maitre d' or waiter in advance that you should receive the bill. If the server gives the bill to your guest ask them for the bill. A simple way to prevent this from happening is to let the server or maitre d' know in advance that the bill should be brought to you. Discretely review the bill. Signal the waiter when you would like to pay by putting the bill holder to the edge of the table, with the bills or the credit card sticking out.
Tell the waiter if you would like them to keep the change. You should prearrange how the bill is being paid by you-cash, card, or other means. Remember to tip your waiter a good amount for moderate service; and a much bigger tip for excellent service.
If there is a problem with the bill, quietly discuss it with the waiter. If the waiter is not cooperative,

excuse yourself from the table and ask to speak to the manager.

If your Credit Card is declined:
Do not call attention to the situation
If your card continues to be declined, and you do not have enough cash to pay, ask to pay by cheque, or visit the nearest ATM, or send through someone or return the next day with cash.
If the restaurant declines these suggestions, you have no option but to return to the table and throw yourself at the mercy of your companions.
Repay their kindness within 24 hours, in cash.

Business Meal Follow-up:
Thank you notes

The Thank You Note
When to send one: A handwritten thank you note must be sent in response to:
- ✓ Gifts- any kind
- ✓ Dinner, parties or get-togethers
- ✓ After a meal outside/ or at their home
- ✓ Congratulations- on a milestone, an event or achievement, job/college interview
- ✓ Contributions made- sponsors of any of your events, fund raiser, etc.
- ✓ Any other time that is appropriate

Remember that it takes only a minute to write a quick note, but the reward is much greater than just a verbal "thank you" or phone call. A thank you note need not be lengthy- its purpose is only to convey gratefulness. Your note should be sent in a timely manner, however better late than never

What should Thank You Notes cover?

A note has two advantages: a) it doesn't interrupt the other person's time 2) it comes across as warmer and more gracious. This is why it is more preferred to a phone call.

It must ideally contain:
- ✓ A formal greeting and salutation
- ✓ A display of gratitude-Something unique, special or memorable about the event, gift or gesture
- ✓ Expressing to the guest how nice it was to dine with him/ her and briefly recapping any business details.

✓ Any details that show that you remember the party/ event and how you had a good time

How should the notes be?
✓ Notes should be sent promptly.
✓ Thank you notes are usually written on a small fold-over note (usually 3 x 5 or 4 x 6) or on a correspondence card (flat card, usually 4 x 6)
✓ If using the fold-over note, write on page 3. If using the correspondence card, write only on the front. Use Blue or Black Ink
✓ Begin with the Greeting: *Dearest Aunt,* Write your appreciation: *The grey sneakers is just amazing. It fits so snug-Appreciate a lot and thank you very much!* Mention its use: *I am sure going to use these to all my college parties.* Look ahead: *I'm looking forward to seeing you soon during the next set of holidays in September. Close: Love always, Cynthia*

Here's a sample:
Dear Sarah,
Thank you for that delicious dinner we had last night. I really appreciate all the trouble you put in, in going out of the way to make Jonathan and myself so at ease.
Most of all were those helpful and powerful inputs that you shared with us that will now enable us have a clearer understanding of the upcoming project that we are so excited to be working along with you. I know together, we will make this a resounding success!
Thank you once again.

Sincerely yours,
Gerard
Title
Company Name (logo)

Reciprocating to the Invitation

When you invite someone to a business lunch, dinner, or breakfast, it does not always mean they are obligated to reciprocate. This is particularly more appropriate to business situations where you are not expected to repay an invitation to a strictly-business meal, no matter who invited you - a customer, a client, or your boss. But you may certainly want to do so if you are looking at continuing business together. So also, it applies to a customer who has been entertained by a salesperson or supplier-is not expected to return the invitation, even if his or her spouse or family was invited.

However, for social settings, you will need to return social invitations from your colleagues, friends and other business associates.

Conclusion

Success may look different for everyone, but practicing good work etiquette, being professional, productive and respectful to people around you will help you achieve your ultimate goal. These skills will not only serve you well now, but also in the future. In today's competitive environment, carrying yourself professionally and managing yourself at the dinner table is an area of expertise that is much sought after.

The Golden Rule of Etiquette is that when you are in doubt; discretely watch until others show the way. Keep in mind that etiquette rules are not commandments- learn the standards and then apply them as you see fit.

When you become comfortable with what you've learned, most of this becomes second nature- completely natural to you. Remember, that knowing most of this information and being sincere, will give you the confidence to tackle all situations ahead of you, so you can concentrate on your business at hand!

And if you do forget some of this, you have one very important rule to remember and fall back on- Always use: Common sense, Respect, Compassion, and Kindness. Always take the higher ground, and do not respond to rudeness with rudeness.

Etiquette is after all, behaving yourself a little better than is absolutely essential... so I wish you well moving further up your career with Great Personal and Professional Success!

About the Author
'GERARD ASSEY'

Gerard Assey is a Graduate in Economics, a PGD in Management (HRD) and holds a Doctorate in Leadership. Gerard holds several International Qualifications in Sales, Debt Collection, Training & Teaching, and is a 'Fellow' of the prestigious 'Institute of Sales & Marketing Management'-UK, a Certified NLP Practitioner, a 'Certified Trainer', an 'Accredited Management Teacher-Behavioral Sciences', a 'Certified Competency Facilitator', a 'Certified Management Consultant'- (the International credentials of a professional management consultant, awarded in accordance with global standards of the ICMCI); and a Certification from the University of Michigan in 'Successful Negotiation: Essential Strategies and Skills'

He is also a Member of the 'National Association of Sales Professionals' backed with several years experience in varied industries, both in India and Overseas. He also holds an 'Etiquette Consultant' Certification from the USA (by Sue Fox, Author of Best Seller: 'Business Etiquette for Dummies'. She has trained some of the top celebrities' world over). He was also a recipient of a scholarship for extensive training in Japan on 'Corporate Management for India'.

Gerard Assey is 'Founder & Chief Corporate Trainer' of the Group: **'Citius, Altius, Fortius Unlimited'**- an organization that **celebrated 20 years of Glorious**

Service in 2021, focusing on 3 Core Competencies: **People. Performance. Profit**; in functional areas of Sales & Marketing, HR & Organizational Development, covering Recruitment, Training & Consultancy!

Having managed organizations with large Sales Forces in India & Overseas, his specialization cover extensive areas of Sales Training (All levels - Presentation, Negotiation, Key/ Strategic Accounts Management & Managerial Skills for all sectors), Bid Proposal/ Capture Planning/ Management Trainings, Retail Sales, Customer Service & Customer Retention Programs, Training for Prevention & Collection of Debt, Self & Personal Development Programs (Time Management, Teamwork & Team Building, Business Etiquette & Personal Grooming, Leadership & Managerial Skills, People Management Skills, Train-the-Trainer etc), including preparation of Custom-designed Business Manuals for Internal (HR, Induction, and Sales etc) & External use (Instruction, User Manuals).

Gerard has successfully conducted over 5900 Trainings & Workshops (as of Nov '22) all across India, Middle East, Africa, Europe & S.E. Asia. Besides public programs conducted regularly, both in India & Overseas, he has some of the top names as clients whom he services from Single Owners to large Public & Government undertakings, covering all sectors, for their in-house needs.

His website: www.CollectionSkills.com is the only one in this part of the world to be featured in the 'Collections & Credit Risk Magazine-USA' under 'Who's Who in Training' and ranks TOP, along with other websites listed below on most search engines.

Gerard is author of 48 books already (as on Nov 2022),

A few of the business related books being:

1. Bite-sized Bits on Commonsense Management
2. Heart to Heart on Life's Principles'
3. How to become a Successful Manager
4. The Sales Professionals' Master Workbook of S.Y.S.T.E.M.S
5. The Professional Business Email Etiquette Handbook & Guide
6. The Professional Business Video-Conferencing Etiquette Handbook & Guide
7. Professional Presentation Skills
8. Exceptional Customer Service
9. Professional Tele-Marketing Skills
10. Professional Debt Collection Skills
11. The G.R.E.A.T. Sales & Service Workbook
12. Sales Training Advantage for Results (*The Ultimate Sales Training Manual to enable you stand out as a S.T.A.R.*)
13. CEO Daily Planner & Organizer
14. The Sales Professionals' Master Daily Planner
15. The Professional Debt Collector's Master Daily Planner
16. My Daily Planner & Organizer
17. MY EMERGENCY INFORMATION RECORD (Family Emergency & Peace of Mind Planner)
18. The Ultimate Therapist & Counselors Planner and Organizer
19. Building an Ethical Workplace
20. Managing Relationships at Work
21. Managing Business Meetings Effectively
22. Effective Delegation Skills
23. Goal Setting for Success
24. B2B Selling by Email
25. Professional Business Etiquette & Grooming
26. Dining Etiquette & Table Manners

Besides regularly contributing to business & trade journals, including international ones such as the 'Creative Training Techniques' and the 'Sales News' of the U.S.A, He is also a member of several prestigious bodies & trade associations, having participated in many Conferences & Workshops in India & Overseas.

Prior to his last assignment of leading & managing a large MNC as head, Gerard had a 3-year stint in the Middle East as a Consultant with a leading British Consultancy Firm.

As the past 'Official Country Representative' for the International Business Award- 'THE STEVIES'-(the business world's own Oscar) for about 4 years- he ensured a few Indian companies that qualify for the same every year!

Gerard can be contacted at:
Email: training@Sales-Training.in,training@CollectionSkills.com
Websites:
    www.Sales-Training.in
    www.EtiquetteWorks.in
    www.CollectionSkills.com
    www.RetailSalesTraining.in
    www.SalesTrainingIndia.com
    www.ManualPreparation.com
    www.TrainingWithPuppets.com
    www.FirstContactAcademy.com
    www.SalesAndMarketingRecruiter.com

Our TRAININGS & BOOKS that can help your team

- ✓ **Sales Effectiveness**: Selling Skills for any Sector: Service/ Logistics/ FMCG Realty/ Insurance & Finance/ Media/ SPA's, Health Clubs & Salons/ Key Account Management, Effective Negotiation Skills/ Bid & Proposal Management Skills/ Retail Sales Training: Any Sector (Auto, Jewelry, Clothing, Luxury etc)
- ✓ **Customer Service Skills**-Complaints Handling & Customer Retention
- ✓ **Debt Prevention & Collection Skills**
- ✓ **Etiquette & Grooming**
- ✓ **Leadership & Managerial Skills**
- ✓ **Self & Personal Development Skills**: Presentation Skills/ Effective Communication Skills/Business Proposal Writing Skills/ Problem Solving & Decision Making Skills/ Empowering Secretaries-The perfect PA! (For Secretaries & PA's)/ Effective Time Management/ Teamwork & Teambuilding/ P.R.I.D.E- **P**ersonal **R**esponsibility **I**n **D**elivering **E**xcellence

Printed in Great Britain
by Amazon

32118311R00056